Magn

Contents

Lesley Wing Jan

RIGBY

What do magnets do?

Magnets can help us do things.

Magnets:

● pick up pins,

● find **metal** in the sand,

● hold notes to
the fridge,

● can be used to
play games.

What are magnets?

Magnets are metals that can pull some things towards them. They can also push some things away.

FACT The bigger the magnet, the stronger it is.

Metals with **iron** in them are pulled towards a magnet. Objects that **cling** to a magnet are **magnetic**.

All these things are magnetic because they have iron in them.

Objects made of plastic, wood or rubber are not magnetic. They won't be pulled to a magnet.

FACT This special stone found in the earth is called **magnetite**. It is a **natural** magnet.

Magnetic force

Magnets are able to pull or push things because they have a special **force**. This force is called a magnetic force.

Watch what happens to these **iron filings**.

① Put a piece of paper over a magnet.

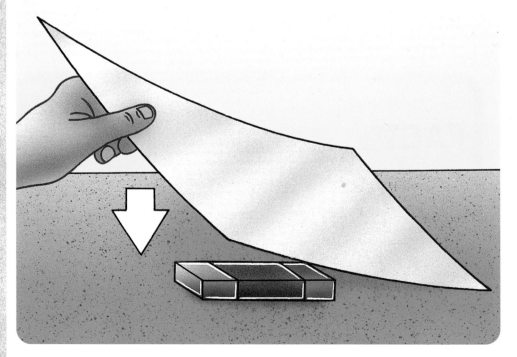

2 Sprinkle the iron filings on the paper. Give the paper a soft tap.

3 The magnet makes the iron filings form a pattern.

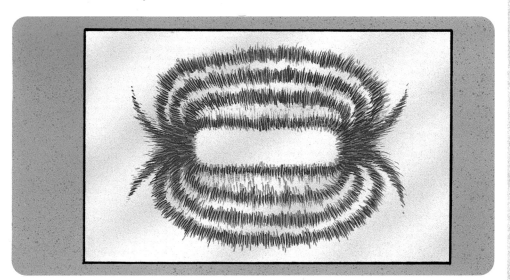

Make a magnet

When some metals touch a magnet, they become magnetic, too.

1 Put a paper clip on a magnet.

2 Add another paper clip to the first paper clip.

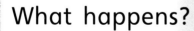

What happens?

3 Each paper clip becomes a magnet.

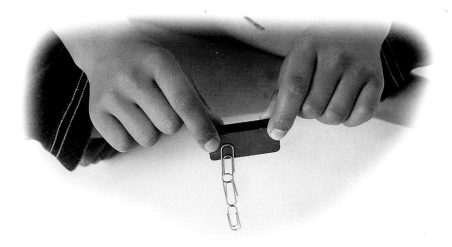

If you take the magnet away, the paper clips will stop being magnets.

Magnet guessing game

Look at these things. Which do you think will be pulled towards a magnet?

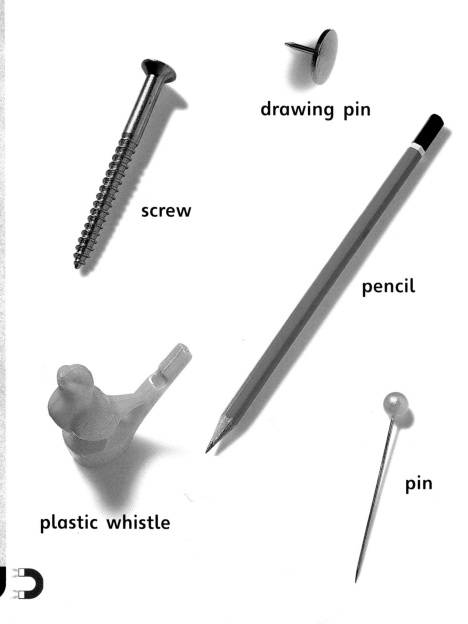

drawing pin

screw

pencil

plastic whistle

pin

nail

note pad

paper clip

eraser

glass bottle

fish hook

crayon

13

Magnetic

screw

nail

pin

drawing pin

fish hook

paper clip

All of these things have iron in them,
so they are magnetic.

eraser
An eraser is made of plastic.

whistle
This whistle is made of plastic.

bottle
This bottle is made of glass.

pencil
A pencil is made of wood and lead.

note pad
A note pad is made of paper.

crayon
A crayon is made of wax.

Glossary

cling	to pull in and hold
force	anything that can cause a push or a pull
iron	a metal
iron filings	tiny pieces of iron
magnetic	able to be made into a magnet
magnetite	a stone that is magnetic
metal	strong, shiny material such as iron and steel
natural	found in or made by nature

Index